WHY
REVIVAL
WAITS

SELWYN HUGHES

WHY REVIVAL WAITS

"If my people who are
called by my name..."

2 CHRONICLES 7:14

BROADMAN
& HOLMAN
PUBLISHERS

NASHVILLE, TENNESSEE

Ten-Digit ISBN: 0–8054–4047–X
Thirteen-Digit ISBN: 978–0–8054–4047–8

Published by Broadman & Holman Publishers
Nashville, Tennessee

Dewey Decimal Classification: 269.24
Subject Heading: REVIVALS \
EVANGELISTIC WORK

Scripture quotations are from the Holy Bible,
New International Version, copyright © 1973,
1978, 1984 by International Bible Society.

Quotes from *God's Answer: Revival Sermons* by
Duncan Campbell are used by permission of The
Faith Mission, Govan House, 2 Drum Street,
Edinburgh EH17 8QG.

1 2 3 4 5 6 7 8 9 10   10 09 08 07 06 05

CONTENTS

CHAPTER 1

What Really Is Revival?

There is, I believe, no greater issue facing the church of Jesus Christ at this time than the subject of Holy Spirit revival. And there is no greater passage in the whole of Scripture that shows the way to revival than 2 Chronicles 7:14—a statement so seemingly simple yet so positively staggering in its implications:

> If my people, who are called by my name,
> will humble themselves and pray and
> seek my face and turn from their wicked
> ways, then will I hear from heaven and
> will forgive their sin and will heal their
> land.

The great Welsh revivalist preachers of past centuries used to refer to this verse regularly in their preaching. Many Christians can recite it at the drop of a hat. It is God's final and finished formula on the subject of revival, his recipe for a spiritual awakening.

Before we focus in detail on this remarkable text, we must take a little time to establish what we mean by *revival*. The word is used loosely in many circles, and there is a tendency to describe revival as a great weekend in which a church sees more numbers than usual coming to know the Lord. The vague way in which the word is thrown around is unhelpful, to say the least.

Jim Packer, professor of historical and systematic theology at Regent College, Vancouver, says on this point: "It seems that any new outburst of activity in the Church, any cloud of dust raised by the stamping of excited feet, will be hailed by somebody as revival."[1]

In the truest sense of the word, *revival* is an unusual and extraordinary movement of God's Spirit that marks it off as being vastly different from the normal sense of God's presence in the church. It is not just a spiritual trickle, a rivulet, or even a river; it is an awesome flood of God's Spirit, a mighty Niagara that sweeps everything before it.

Sometimes in attempting to define what something is, it is useful to begin by defining what it is not. So, in seeking to understand revival, let's start by looking at it first from that perspective.

Revival Is Not a Great Evangelistic Thrust

When Billy Graham came to Britain in the 1950s, thousands of people were converted and committed their lives to Jesus Christ. Some of the Christian newspapers at that time stated: "Revival has come to Britain," but wonderful though those days were, it was not revival—at least not in the real sense of the word. It was a demonstration of God-anointed and effective evangelism, but it did not deserve the description of real revival.

Evangelism and revival are quite different. Evangelism is the expression of the church; revival is an experience in the church. In evangelism the preacher calls on people to get saved; in revival people often call on the preacher to tell them how they can be saved. In Wales during the 1904 revival it was not unusual for people to interrupt whoever was preaching by shouting out from the congregation: "What must we do to be saved?" or "I need to find peace for my heart . . . help me please."

My grandfather, who witnessed the Welsh revival, reported to me an account of a meeting he was at in the little town of Merthyr Tydfil, Mid Glamorgan, during the year 1904. A preacher, well known for his style of focusing in the first part of his sermon on the law of God before turning in the second part to the subject of grace, noticed after the first twenty minutes of his sermon a number of people leaving the church in tears. He asked one of the deacons to find out what was the matter with them. When the deacon went outside, he found them leaning against the walls of the church in great distress.

"What is wrong?" he asked. One of them replied, "We just couldn't sit through any more preaching on the law of God and we are waiting until the preacher turns from the law to grace—then we will go in and hope to find salvation for our souls." Through powerful evangelistic preaching people can come under great conviction of sin at any time, but where the Spirit is present in awesome power as in revival, then the conviction of sin and the desire for righteousness are deeper than it is sometimes possible to imagine.

Revival Is Not the Restoration of Large Numbers of Backslidden Christians

It's wonderful to see the thawing of the frost of indifference in the hearts of God's people, when the grave clothes of decorum are changed for the garments of praise, when voices seldom heard in testimony tell of God's wondrous grace, and when lips long sealed begin to speak or sing his praises. But this in itself is not revival.

I preached in a church some years ago that, according to its pastor, had been in the spiritual doldrums for well over a decade. Prior to the weeklong meetings that I conducted, the pastor said, "I have to say that most of the congregation here are thoroughly backslidden, they rarely read their Bibles, no more than two or three come to the weekly prayer meetings, they appear like one of the churches in the book of Revelation to have lapsed into nominalism, having a name that they live but showing little evidence of spiritual life."

One night during that week the Holy Spirit swept through the congregation in a powerful way. Hundreds recommitted themselves to Jesus Christ, staying at the church to pray until well past midnight. The following night the whole atmosphere in the church was so different that the pastor said, "This feels like revival." Rededications to Christ numbered during that week came close to five hundred. It was indeed a wonderful and remarkable move of the Holy Spirit but, again, it could not truly be classified as revival.

Revival Is Not Unusually Powerful and Exciting Meetings

Powerful and exciting meetings give us a taste of revival, of course. In the almost sixty years I have been a Christian, I have seen some wonderful things happen and sat through some thrilling meetings. The most memorable of these was in Pusan, South Korea, in the late 1970s. I was conducting a crusade there and was invited to speak at a 5:00 a.m. prayer meeting where I was told five thousand Christians met to spend time with God before setting out on their day's work.

Just after the meeting began the Holy Spirit fell in a way I have not experienced before or since. You might remember in the Acts of the Apostles there was an occasion where the place in which Christians had gathered to pray was shaken (Acts 4:31). I cannot vouch for the fact that the building in which we met that midweek morning to pray was literally shaken, but it seemed to almost everyone present that such was the case.

There was such a tremendous atmosphere of God's presence in the place that it was impossible for me to get up and preach. The Koreans have a wonderful way of what they call "praying in concert," when everyone prays out loud, asking God for whatever is on their hearts. Then after they have prayed they lift their voices in powerful praise.

It was during this prolonged time of praise that I heard a Korean woman who was standing near me speaking words of praise to God in the Welsh language. Although I am not a fluent Welsh speaker, I clearly understood what she was saying. In perfect Welsh she was praising God in words that, when translated, said this: "Thank you, Lord, for the gift of your salvation . . . for giving your Son for us on the cross of Calvary . . . for the gift of your Holy Spirit . . ." and so on.

The effect on me was so great that I felt goose bumps coming up on my flesh as I stood surrounded by these thousands of worshipping Koreans, praising God in their own language—and some, no doubt, in other languages inspired by the Spirit as well.

I consider the weeks I spent in Korea to be the closest I have ever come in my life to real revival.

I corresponded later with those who had invited me to Korea. They reported that though God continued to bless them in a wonderful way, they had not experienced anything similar to the level we had encountered that particular morning. It was a taste of revival, but it was not sustained enough to be called the real thing.

What, Then, Is Revival?

If the situations I have mentioned are not revival, then what is? Although I have been talking and writing about revival for most of my Christian life, when it comes to defining it I come up against the same difficulty as an old friend of mine who said, "Revival in a definition is like David in Saul's armor; it just doesn't seem to fit." When we have said all we can say about revival, it remains one of heaven's greatest mysteries.

However, as a start, let's look at the diction-ary definition of the word. My *Encarta* dictionary says revival is the "process of bringing back something to life, to full consciousness or full strength," suggesting that something is alive but is about to die.

Years ago, when I was a pastor in Llandeilo, West Wales, I visited an old lady, a member of my church, who was very ill and appeared to be at death's door. Her sister who was looking after her said, "I doubt whether she has long for this world." Although she was semiconscious I prayed for her and the family. As I left I remem-ber thinking to myself maybe that would be the last time I would see her alive.

Imagine my surprise a week later when she skipped up behind me in a local shop, tapped me on the shoulder, and said, "They tell me I have been at death's door, but two days ago something wonderful happened, and now I feel as good if not better than I have ever felt." She had revived!

It is inappropriate, I believe (as we said earlier), to apply the word *revival* to people being converted. Those who come to Christ for conversion don't experience revival; they experience resurrection. Revival refers to the flaming forth once again of love for the Lord in those who, having known the truth and experienced the life of God in their souls, had grown cold.

Revival is one of those "concertina" words that, in use, keeps alternating between a narrower and broader sense. In its narrowest sense, it can be applied to the personal quickening of the life of an individual when he or she has an unusual and extraordinary encounter with the Holy Spirit. In its broadest sense, it can be applied to a community of believers who have been supernaturally revitalized at every level of their corporate existence—their inner life and the way they relate to one another and the outside world. It is with corporate revival that I am mainly concerned in this book.

While it was necessary to begin with a dictionary definition of the word *revival* (for communication breaks down when we give meanings to words that are not consistent with their true definitions), we must look outside the dictionary for a true description of spiritual revival. Some of my favorite descriptions I have come across in my time are these:

> Revival is the inrush of divine life into a body threatening to become a corpse.
> **D. M. Panton**

> Revival is God bending down to the dying embers of a fire just about to go out and breathing into it until it bursts again into flame.
> **Christmas Evans**

> Revival is waking up to the fact that you are asleep.
> **David Thomas**

My favorite description of revival, however, is the simple but sublime statement given by Dr. Martyn Lloyd-Jones:

> Revival is the church returning to Pentecost.

Whenever I think of the church returning to Pentecost there comes to mind the story of Billy Graham, who, as a young Youth for Christ evangelist, held a citywide tent crusade in Los Angeles, California, in 1949. Thousands of people came to Christ during that crusade, many of them Hollywood film stars.

A minister who belonged to a liberal church in the city (liberalism is the mind-set that puts human thoughts above God's thoughts) wrote in the local paper, "Billy Graham has put the church in Los Angeles back 100 years." When he heard that, Billy is said to have responded, "Oh dear—I was really trying to put it back 2,000 years."

At Pentecost, a high-voltage burst of spiritual energy and supernatural power flowed into the midst of those early disciples such as had never been known before. In a comparatively short time, it affected the whole nation, spilling over eventually to other nations, even as far away as Europe. When the church witnesses the same degree of power that was present at Pentecost and that power spreads to whole communities, even to a nation as it did in Wales, then and only then can it be said to be revival.

Wales (of which I am a native) has often been described as the land of revivals, as there have been repeated stirrings of the Spirit in the nation, especially between the seventeenth and early twentieth centuries. It would be wrong in my view, and limiting to the Holy Spirit, for the church to expect any future revival to have the exact historical precedents of the past, but there are several elements of revival that have to be present in order for it to be classified as true revival.

Our Welsh theologians used to say the three great characteristics of classic revival are these:

1. An intense, palpable, and extraordinary sense of God's presence.

2. A deep desire to be rid of all sin.
3. A powerful impact on the wider community.

When revival came to Wales in 1904, all three of these were in evidence.

There was an intense, palpable, and extraordinary sense of God's presence throughout almost the whole of the principality during that astonishing year, and it lingered for some time afterwards. People would become aware of God's presence, even deep down in the mines, and cry out to be saved. There are stories of blaspheming miners struck down by God's power and then, after surrendering their lives to Christ, rising to find that so deep was the work of the Spirit in their hearts, they no longer wanted to swear.

This sometimes created problems for those who directed the pit ponies that hauled the tiny trucks of coal from the coal face to the cages that came down to the pit bottom, because their instructions to the ponies were often given through swear words. Many of those who were converted in this way tell how, following their conversion, they had to teach their horses a new language. As one wag put it, "On such occasions down there in the bowels of the earth, even the horses knew there was revival!"

There was also a great desire in people's hearts to be rid of sin. *Ysbryd Glan* is the Welsh term for the Holy Spirit that translated literally means "clean or pure spirit." During the days of revival people could be heard crying out again and again in their native language, "O God, make me clean." To quote Jim Packer again: "No upsurge of religious interest or excitement merits the name . . . if there is no deep sense of sin at its heart. God's coming and the consequent impact of His Word makes Christians more sensitive to sin than they previously were; consciences become tender and a profound humbling takes place."[2]

The conviction of sin was very much part of the early Christian church. In Acts 2:37–41, for example, we read that those who listened to the apostle Peter were "cut [pierced] to their heart" with a sense of guilt for Jesus' death.

Then the impact on the wider community was such that a community conscience informed by Christian values emerged. Revival, wherever it happens, usually has an ethical overspill into the world. There was a respect for law and order. In the Welsh valleys throughout 1904, crime figures dropped, and for some months many magistrates found they had no cases to consider. They were presented with white gloves as a symbol of the "clean" communities.

Most of those who have studied the subject of revival, or indeed who have experienced it, appear to agree with this analysis of the Welsh theologians. Duncan Campbell was greatly used by God in the Hebrides revival in the early 1950s. When asked, "What have been the outstanding features of the Hebrides revival?" Campbell answered, "Three things stand out clearly. First, an awareness of God. . . . The second main feature has been deep conviction of sin. . . . Physical manifestations and prostrations have been a further feature." He also commented on the fact that there was a tremendous impact on the community, revival leaping the boundaries of the parish bringing refreshing and spiritual life to many all over the island.[3]

In relation to a powerful awareness of God, he said:

> I have known men out on the fields, others at their weaving looms, so overcome by the sense of God that they were found prostrate on the ground. Here are the words of one who felt the hand of God upon him: "The grass beneath my feet and the rocks around me seem to cry, 'flee to Christ for refuge.'" This supernatural illumination of the Holy Spirit led many in this revival to a saving knowledge of the Lord Jesus Christ before they came near to any meeting connected with the movement. I have no hesitation in saying that this awareness of God is the crying need of the Church today; "the fear of the Lord is the beginning of wisdom"; but this cannot be worked up by any human effort, it must come down.[4]

Many critics claim that the reports of past revivals are often exaggerated and idealized, and there is no doubt that in some cases this is true. However, as a number of people in my family were impacted greatly by the 1904 revival and were firsthand observers of the great things that God did, I have been able to check with these reliable sources in relation to some of the stories I have reported above.

You may wonder why I have spent so much time focusing on the meaning of revival. It is for this reason:

I am concerned that unless we have a clear understanding of what revival is and what it is all about we may easily settle for less than God wants to give us.

Why Do We Need Revival?

The history of the Christian church is not one long uninterrupted scene of manifest divine power. Even in the days of the early church, six out of the seven churches in the book of Revelation had quenched the Spirit so much that they had to be severely reprimanded by the Lord Jesus Christ.

Look at the state of the contemporary Christian church in Great Britain. Yes, there are some good things happening, but the fact is Christianity in the mainstream churches is declining. According to Peter Brierley, a reliable research expert, we are losing about one thousand young people a week. The level of spiritual energy in the contemporary Christian church seems no match for the fast-developing agnosticism of this postmodern generation. And while Christianity appears to be declining, non-Christian religions are growing and developing at an astonishing rate.

In today's Britain there are more Muslims than Methodists, and the way Buddhism is growing who knows but one day there may be more Buddhists than Baptists. And this is what was once called a Christian country. While we must be thankful for the good things that are happening such as Spring Harvest, Alpha, and the large summer conferences that draw thousands of Christians, we have to confess that, generally speaking, after several decades of charismatic renewal we are making about as much impact on the nation as a peashooter on the rock of Gibraltar.

Something much bigger and more powerful is needed if the spiritual situation is to be redeemed. It is going to take something much more than our methods and techniques to turn things around spiritually. As I see it, revival is the only answer.

CHAPTER 2

Why Then Does It Not Come?

I think I see something of the answer in the text I introduced to you at the start— 2 Chronicles 7:14. For years after coming into the ministry I looked at this text wishing I had enough nerve to preach on it. I used to think that to try and expound it would spoil it—like picking to pieces a rose to show off its beauty.

My two favorite verses in the whole of Scripture are John 3:16 and 2 Chronicles 7:14. John 3:16 says almost everything that needs to be said about the way to salvation, and

2 Chronicles 7:14 says almost everything that needs to be said about the way to revival.

David Thomas, one of my spiritual mentors, an eloquent preacher (and also an uncle of mine), used to say of 2 Chronicles 7:14: "This great text, lying like a diamond on a velvet couch, never ceases to glisten and glitter as the light of the Holy Spirit falls upon it." Ever since I heard him say that, every time I look at or think about this text that is the picture I have in my mind—a spiritual diamond that, under the light of the Holy Spirit, sparkles with truths that if heeded show us the way to a deeper relationship with God. If we do not see it in that way, perhaps the reason is our eyes are more dazzled by the glare of this world than with the "precious stone" itself.

Permit me to stay with this image of a diamond for a moment. Years ago one could see in a shop window in Regent Street, London, an exact replica of all the great diamonds of the world before they were cut. They looked like dull misshapen lumps of glass. How different, however, after the expert (called a lapidary) goes to work on a diamond and begins to cut faces on it so that its beauty might be better seen. Cutting faces on a diamond is called faceting, and it is true to say that apart from this highly-skilled work, the beauty and loveliness of the stone would never be seen by the human eye. Someone who has observed the work of diamond cutting firsthand has written this:

> When a lapidary cuts a stone he always
> cuts to a pattern. It needs hardly to be
> said that he does not take the stone rough
> and cut three or four facets unrelated to
> one another. There is a design in his
> mind. The cutting itself is a work of art.
> The light that shoots out from the several
> faces when his work is done dazzles and
> delights the eye of all who really look.[1]

What I want to do now is not so much expound 2 Chronicles 7:14 but turn it word by word and phrase by phrase so that "the light shoots out from its several faces." My prayer is that this great text will do for you what it has done for me—set your heart on fire for revival.

It begins with the preposition *if.*

"If"

Just as great doors swing open on small hinges, so this little word *if* unfolds for us the truth that whatever part God plays in a spiritual reawakening, we have a part to play too.

In the main there are two opposing schools of thought in relation to revival. There are those who say revival is a sovereign act of God and cannot be predicted or procured through any human means. Others say the church can enter into revival anytime it wants to—providing it is prepared to pay the price. Charles Finney, one of the strongest proponents of the latter view, claimed that self-examination and earnest prayer on the part of a congregation would always secure a divine visitation. "Revival," he said on one occasion, "is no more a miracle than a crop of wheat . . . a farmer sows and wheat comes up."

As with most opposing theories, the truth usually lies somewhere in the middle. When I was a student of theology I learned this: "There are two rails laid down in Scripture—one is God's sovereignty and the other is human responsibility. If you do away with human responsibility, you have nothing to save; if you do away with God's sovereignty, you have nothing to save with. The Bible will not make sense to you unless you are prepared to run on both of those rails."

What does it mean when we talk about the sovereignty of God and human responsibility in relation to the subject of revival? We mean by God's sovereignty that he takes action when he sees fit and answers our prayers at his own speed and in his own good time. In every revival throughout history, men and women have stood back and said words similar to these: "This is the Lord's doing, and it is marvelous in our eyes."

However, divine sovereignty does not relieve us of our human responsibility. There are things that we need to do to bring revival closer. Christmas Evans, one of our Welsh revivalists, put it well when he said, "Revival comes from God, but it is borne to earth on the wings of fervent, believing prayer." Duncan Campbell said something similar when he wrote, "God is the God of revival, but men and women are the agents through whom revival is made possible." The Almighty delights to team up with his people. We could not experience revival without him, and he won't bring it about without us.

The word *if* is clearly a word of condition. "If anyone is thirsty," said Jesus on one occasion, "let him come to me and drink" (John 7:37). And again, "But if you do not forgive men their sins, your Father will not forgive your sins" (Matt. 6:15). The Bible fairly bulges with texts in which God implies that if we will do this, he will do that. So, clearly, right at the start, some responsibility is placed at our door.

We are bidden over and over again in Scripture that whenever we find ourselves in need of spiritual reawakening, we are to admit our lapsed condition, repent of it, and open ourselves up to God for him to restore us to where we should be.

This brief selection of Scriptures puts the truth most clearly:

> Sow for yourselves righteousness, reap the
> fruit of unfailing love, and break up your
> unplowed ground; for it is time to seek
> the LORD, until he comes and showers
> righteousness on you.
>
> **Hosea 10:12**

> "Yet I hold this against you: You have for-
> saken your first love. Remember the
> height from which you have fallen!
> Repent and do the things you did at first.
> If you do not repent, I will come to you
> and remove your lampstand from its
> place."
>
> **Revelation 2:4–5**

> "Call to me and I will answer you and tell
> you great and unsearchable things you do
> not know."
>
> **Jeremiah 33:3**

"Return, faithless people; I will cure you
of backsliding."

Jeremiah 3:22

Take words with you and return to the
LORD. Say to him: "Forgive all our sins
and receive us graciously, that we may
offer the fruit of our lips."

Hosea 14:2

But to whom is God speaking when he says,
"If"? Listen carefully.

"If My People"

The message of revival is not for everyone; it
is aimed specifically at the people of God. The
responsibility for facing up to the challenge of
revival is not on those outside the church, but on
those inside the church. That is you and me—if
you are a believing Christian.

One of the things I have observed among
those with an interest in revival is a tendency
with some to focus more on the desperate spiritual state of the nation than the low spiritual

state of the church. Now every Christian ought to have a deep concern about the moral condition of our nation. We ought to lament the fact that our country is in a bad way spiritually and morally.

Every year we kill millions of babies in the womb, we treat the Ten Commandments as if they were a joke, we consider education to be the means of our salvation, we allow our airwaves to carry the most poisonous and pernicious images, we make it possible for homosexuals to go through a form of marriage, there is corruption in high places, our courts are slow to punish evildoers, teenage pregnancies are alarmingly high, things are happening in our nation—terrible things—that cry out to high heaven.

And while we lament the spiritual state of our land we must surely be aware that there is a worldwide epidemic of corruption, sleaze, and moral deterioration that covers the earth. Selflessness has given way to an epidemic of "what's in it for me?" and self-interest seems part and parcel of life—particularly political life.

Paul Harvey read the following statement on his radio program:

There is an organization in the USA consisting of 600 people:

20 have been accused of spousal abuse

7 have been arrested for fraud

10 for writing bad checks

17 bankrupted for 2 businesses—at least

3 arrested for assault

71 couldn't get a credit card

14 arrested on drug-related charges

8 arrested for shoplifting

21 involved in lawsuits

84 stopped for being over the alcohol limit while driving.

The name of that organization? The House of Congress.

I wonder what a similar survey of other governments would reveal? Surely in the light of these things we Christians must carry a prayerful concern for the state of our nation and the world, but before we get carried away with the need for greater character qualities in the lives of those who lead our nation, let us not miss the point that when it comes to revival that is not where we should start.

Our strongest criticism and our deepest concern must be reserved for ourselves. God is concerned with the state of our nation, but he has an equal if not greater concern for his people, you and me.

To start by lamenting the deplorable spiritual state of our nation is to begin at the wrong end. The initial focus should be on ourselves— what kind of people we are and what kind of people we should be. We are quick to point out the sins of non-Christians, but not so quick to look at our own sins. Revival starts with the people of God.

But is God talking to all men and women who call themselves Christians when he says, "My people"? No. For there are many who call themselves "Christians" but have never had a personal encounter with Jesus Christ. God put this matter beyond all doubt in 2 Chronicles 7:14.

"If My People Who Are Called by My Name"

And who are those who are called by his name? Those who have first called on his name. Scripture says, "And everyone who calls on the name of the Lord will be saved" (Acts 2:21). If you haven't called on the name of the Lord in a personal way, then, lovingly I say, you cannot claim to be one of his people. You can go to church, live a life that is well within the law, be religious, even take Holy Communion, but if you have not called on him personally, then you are not part of the family of God.

You see, going to church does not make you a Christian any more than going to the theater makes you an actor. God chooses to begin with his own church when he offers revival, and that puts upon us an enormous responsibility. Not one person, but all his people—his true people, that is.

It is a tremendous responsibility to belong to the people of God. Every one of us carries a responsibility for the honor of God's name. As one London preacher from a past generation put it:

> People judge the church by the impression that we make upon them. If a Christian lapses and fails, people don't say to themselves, "That person is an exception"; they judge everyone by the one individual they know who failed. They don't see us as one of hundreds of millions. They observe our ways and they say to themselves . . . if that is what Christianity is all about then I want nothing to do with it. I'm missing nothing. If on the other hand when we are unselfish and loving then they are affected in this way and think of others like that also.[2]

Many Christians are not very wise in the way they relate to others. I spent a weekend preaching in a church in the southwest of England some time ago. I stayed with a very friendly couple, and on Sunday morning the man said, "It's such a nice day, let's not bother with the car, we'll walk to church."

As we set out, he said, "You might be interested to see what will happen as we walk to church this morning. Because I am a Christian many of my neighbors go out of their way to avoid me." He pointed to one up ahead who had just come out of a newsagent's shop obviously buying his Sunday paper and said, "Now watch what he will do as soon as he catches sight of me."

Sure enough, as soon as the neighbor spotted my friend, he went back inside the shop. A few minutes later we came across another neighbor who, when he caught sight of us, crossed to the other side of the road. At this point my curiosity got the better of me, and I said, "How has all this come about?"

"It's simply because when I first moved here I witnessed to my neighbors that I was a Christian."

"And how did you do that?" I asked.

He replied, "I began my witness by saying to them: 'Good morning, do you know you are going to hell?'"

It is one thing when we are ostracized because of Christ; it is another thing when Christ is ostracized because of us. I say again: it is a tremendous responsibility to belong to the people of God. It is not surprising when we consider how foolish are the ways of God's people that the Almighty chooses to begin with his own church when he focuses on revival.

Before we go any further, let me deal with a difficulty that may be in some people's minds concerning the application of this Old Testament Scripture to New Testament times. I have heard it said: "You can't take a verse like this that meant for the nation of Israel and apply it to the church of the present day." My answer to that objection is that while it is true that it is sometimes inappropriate to apply some Old Testament texts to New Testament situations, that does not apply in this case.

Take, for example, the concept of "the people of God" that we have just been discussing. That's a concept that is found everywhere in Scripture. God had a redeemed people in the Old Testament whom he called Israel, and he has a redeemed people in the New Testament called the church. And take the other concepts found in the text that we shall look at in more detail in a moment—concepts such as humility, prayer, intercession, and repentance—these are all truths that are enunciated most clearly in the New Testament and apply to every generation of God's people.

I believe 2 Chronicles 7:14 has as much application to the church of the New Testament as it did to God's people in the Old Testament.

CHAPTER 3

Managing Without God

We turn the jewel again to let the light fall on yet another phrase from 2 Chronicles 7:14: "If my people who are called by my name shall humble themselves . . ."

How do we humble ourselves? Well, first let's think about what exactly humility is, for there are many fallacies in the Christian church about what constitutes this important spiritual quality. Some think that humility is self-effacement, but self-effacement can be a way of gaining face, like Uriah Heep in Charles Dickens's novel *David Copperfield* who approached David Copperfield, wringing his hands and saying, "I am so very 'umble, Master Copperfield . . . so very 'umble."

In a church of which I was once the pastor I remember giving an address on the subject of humility. Afterwards a woman came up to me and said, "I did so much enjoy your address. Humility has always been a favorite topic of mine. In fact I regard it to be one of my best qualities."

Humility has several characteristics. First, it is a right estimation of yourself. You are not God, but you are not a worm either. Humble people see themselves as they really are. Humility also has within it the fact of self-forgetfulness. The humble turn their attention from themselves to God; they rarely think about themselves at all. Again, humility recognizes that without God we can do nothing. Those who are not humble foolishly believe that without them God can do nothing.

Often what we think is humility is really, when put under critical examination, nothing more than self-belittlement. People will often express derogatory opinions of themselves, hoping they are being seen as humble, while deep down in their hearts is the half-conscious hope that someone will contradict them.

In the days when I used to conduct evangelistic crusades in different cities and countries, I had a friend who played the piano for me; he suffered from a strong inferiority complex. He used to persuade himself that this was in fact humility, and I tried several times to disabuse him of this erroneous idea. I made some strides one evening when after a particularly effective meeting I turned to him and said, "That was wonderful playing tonight."

He thought for a moment and said, "No, not really, it wasn't all that good."

"Come on now," I said, "it was tremendous playing—really brilliant."

He said again, "No, I don't think so, not really."

After we had repeated these same sentences to each other a few times I realized what he was doing—he was deliberately putting himself down so that I would lift him up. He thought he was being humble, but in actual fact he was simply belittling himself. I waited for an opportunity to point that out to him, and it came when he said, "Well, it wasn't me, it was the Lord."

"Now come on," I said, "it wasn't that good." He got the point.

Pride: The Most Deadly Sin

Humility, I believe, is best understood when we look at its opposite—pride. I am indebted to C. S. Lewis for this powerful statement concerning pride:

> If you want to know how much pride you
> have, ask yourself how much you dislike
> it in others. If you think you're not con-
> ceited, it means that you are very con-
> ceited indeed; first step toward acquiring
> humility is to realize that one is proud.
> We are all full of pride but we can't see it.
> It blinds us to our own condition. So it is
> wise to admit it even though you do not
> see it or feel it. There can be no surer

41

proof of a confirmed pride than a belief
that one is sufficiently humble.[1]

Did you know that pride was the first sin to
be seen in the universe? That's how the devil
came into being. Once he was an angel of beauty
and delight, but he became puffed up by pride.
Daniel Rowlands, another famous Welsh revivalist, said, "We most resemble the devil when we
are proud, and we most resemble Christ when
we are humble."

"God who thrust out a proud angel from
heaven," said Charles Spurgeon to his students,
"will not tolerate a proud preacher either. God
hides from the proud, you won't even feel him
near you." He drew the attention of his students
to this verse: "Though the LORD is on high, he
looks upon the lowly, but the proud he knows
from afar" (Ps. 138:6).

Is it possible that there could be more pride in
the church you attend than in a comparable group
of non-Christians? Pride in the fact you are saved
and others are not, pride in your knowledge of the
Bible, your ability to pray or preach?

Pride, or the lack of humility, is one of the roots of sin. After all, what is sin? Chop off the first two letters and last two letters, and what are you left with? *I*—the perpendicular pronoun, as someone has called it. See it standing there on the page, *I*, tall and starched and stiff. Sin is really the ego standing up to its full height in the place that God has reserved for himself— the center of the soul.

What does God mean when, in talking about humility, he commands us to humble ourselves? I believe that what he has in mind primarily is a willingness to judge and evaluate ourselves, not by the standards of others, but by the standards of God's Word, the Bible, to come under its authority and submit to its truths. It is not possible to understand what humility is unless we are prepared to lay our lives alongside the Bible.

One of the alarming trends in today's Christian society is the disappearance of the truly biblical Christian. I refer not so much to respecting the Bible as God's Book, or even carrying a Bible to church. I am thinking of those who fail to bring their lives under its authority, to see it for what it is—God's infallible Word—and live by its standards, eager to obey its commands. Such Christians are fast disappearing. We need the attitude that will not stand in judgment over the Scriptures but will sit under them in humility.

Listen to what God, speaking through Isaiah, says: "This is the one I esteem: he who is humble and contrite in spirit, and trembles at my word" (Isa. 66:2). What does it mean to tremble at God's Word? I remember in a counseling session many years ago talking to a young man—a Christian—who had come to me for some spiritual advice over a certain issue but seemed to resist every scriptural principle I presented to him. After an hour or two of this I said, "Look, on your way out of here today I am going to put my Bible down and invite you to walk over it, to wipe your feet on it." He was quite shocked and asked me to explain what I meant.

"Well," I said, "you seem to be unwilling to act on the principles of God's Word that you asked me to show to you, and so you might as well demonstrate your contempt for it by wiping your feet on it." When I said that he began to tremble physically.

I do not usually resort to such melodramatic statements when I am counseling, but in this case it seemed appropriate. I can tell you the counseling session took a decidedly different direction from that moment, and I am glad to say the young man came to a place where he decided to put God's Word into action as it related to his difficulties.

I am not suggesting that the phrase "to tremble at God's Word" means a literal physical trembling. It means, I believe, that we allow the Word, which is alive, to penetrate our lives to such a degree that we feel the inner vibrations of truth in our soul that point out some violation in our life. How many of us can honestly say that we value the Word of God so highly that when we realize we are in violation of it, our soul trembles within us?

It is here then when we talk about pride and the need to step down from it in true humility that we come face to face with the first reason why revival waits.

I have no hesitation in saying that pride or lack of humility is the biggest single impediment to revival. Theologians in the past listed what they called the seven most deadly sins, and what was at the head of that list? Not lust, not cruelty, not even murder. Pride.

Pride is the implacable enemy of God, and he gives some stern warnings in Scripture concerning it—none more sober than this: "God opposes the proud but gives grace to the humble" (James 4:6).

There is a spawning effect about pride that appears in no other sin. It is so vile and loathsome that it makes other sins more vile and loathsome. If pride is the biggest impediment to revival, then it begs the question: What are we going to do about it? How willing are we to bring our lives under the authority of Scripture and face the first of the divine challenges laid out in 2 Chronicles 7:14?

Charles Swindoll in one of his books tells the story of a medical doctor, Evan O'Neill of Kane Summit Hospital in New York City, who operated on himself and removed his appendix while under local anesthesia. Apparently the operation was a success, and his recovery progressed faster than that usually expected of patients who were given general anaesthesia.[2]

It is clear from what God is telling us in 2 Chronicles 7:14 that he is looking to us to operate on ourselves. Let's call it "self-exploratory surgery of the soul." While you are fully conscious, fully aware, I invite you to allow the Holy Spirit to assist you, handing you the only instrument you need to do soul surgery—the germ-free scalpel of Scripture. For what we come to now is this—Hebrews 4:12–13 tells us that "the word of God is living and active. Sharper than any double-edged sword, it penetrates even to dividing soul and spirit, joints and marrow; it judges the thoughts and attitudes of the heart. Nothing in all creation is hidden from God's sight. Everything is uncovered and laid bare before the eyes of him to whom we must give account."

With this reliable instrument, the Word of God, in your hand, take an honest look into your soul and consider how much pride still lies within you. For some it will be your first ever look, for others not the first, but perhaps one long overdue.

Self-exploratory surgery should always be conducted in the presence of God and with the Word of God, in the realization that God is not against us for our sin but for us against our sin. And remember C. S. Lewis's words, that if you think you are not proud, then most likely you are.

Why Does Revival Tarry?

The primary reason is this: we are unwilling to humble ourselves. During the Welsh revival, one of the songs that was sung over and over again, sometimes moving people to deep emotion, was this: "Bend me lower, bend me lower, bend me lower, lower down at Jesus' feet."

Why did they ask God to bend them lower (in other words to humble them) when the Almighty told them in 2 Chronicles 7:14 to humble themselves? Were they going against Scripture here? I think not. They were recognizing that the development of humility is not a mere matter of will power. In all things spiritual there is a merging of the divine and human. We provide the willingness; he provides the power.

Keep that in mind always whenever you conduct any self-exploratory surgery. You need another will working alongside your own. We must come to God with willingness but not depending only on our willingness. We must link ourselves also to his power. The psalmist understood this when he prayed in Psalm 139:23: "Search me, O God, and know my heart; test me and know my anxious thoughts."

CHAPTER 4

CALL ME WHEN
THE FIRE FALLS

The text of 2 Chronicles 7:14 continues: "Shall humble themselves and pray . . ."

You may be feeling somewhat relieved as we move away from the subject of pride, and you may think to yourself: *Well, I may have some pride in me, but here is a test I can pass—I do pray.*

Do you?

How much?

How sincerely?

When, for example, did you last stay up late just to pray? When did you rise early simply to pray?

It is prayer that opens us to God's power. All around us the power of God is flowing, and it comes in at the place of prayer. A little prayer, and a little of that power gets through. A lot of prayer, and a lot comes through. Fervent believing prayer causes it to come in like a flood.

How selfish sometimes are our prayer lives! It's interesting how, when our family is in trouble or our needs cry out to be met, we can develop a passion in prayer that is not there for those who may be outside our small circle. A lot of our praying is shot through with self-interest, our concerns, our needs, and so often everything that comes up has a self axis. Me! Me! Me!

The chief librarian in Dagenham in Essex discovered this prayer among the papers of John Ward, member of parliament for Hackney during the eighteenth century:

> O Lord, Thou knowest I have mine estates
> in the City of London and likewise that
> I have lately purchased an estate in the
> County of Essex. I beseech Thee to pre-
> serve the two counties of Middlesex and
> Essex from fire and earthquake, and, as

I have a mortgage in Hertfordshire, I beg
Thee likewise to have an eye of compas-
sion on that county. For the rest of the
counties, Thou mayest deal with them as
Thou art pleased . . .[1]

It's surprising the strange ideas that some
Christians have in relation to prayer. I have met
many who view it as nothing more than just
reciting what we call the Lord's Prayer. That is an
important framework for understanding what
prayer is all about, and it has been a blessing to
the church universal when said corporately. But
if we think that when we have recited the Lord's
Prayer that is the end of the matter, then we are
just fooling ourselves.

Some Christians have the idea also that it is
no good praying unless you "feel like it." The
precise opposite is nearer the truth. Our prayers
are often more effective when we pray even
though we don't feel like praying. And it is not
difficult to understand why. When we pray
because we feel like it, there is often a degree of
pleasure that we give ourselves. It feels good to
hear our own voice putting together words that

address the Almighty God, to sense a flexibility of language as our tongue becomes like "the pen of a ready writer." We can feel good about ourselves when we pray like that.

When, however, we pray though we do not feel like it, we bring to God not only the content of our prayer but the evidence of a disciplined spirit. We have gone to him against our natural inclination. We have displeased ourselves in order to please him. Prayer is too important to depend on the vagary of feelings. Feelings fluctuate with our health, the weather, the news, circumstances, what we eat, and whom we met last. Our commerce with heaven cannot be conducted on things so fortuitous as that.

Forbes Robinson, himself a man of prayer, said: "Do not mind about feelings. You may have beautiful feelings. Thank God if you have. He sends them. You may have none. Thank God if you have not, for He has kept them back. We do not want to feel better and stronger; we want to be better and stronger."

If in times past you have prayed only when you felt like it, then pause once more for a moment of self-exploratory surgery. Determine to go to God whether you feel like it or not. You would not fail to keep an appointment with an important fellow human being because the inclination had ebbed when the appointed hour came. Courtesy would carry you there if desire didn't. Can you be less courteous with God?

But what kind of praying is it that God is thinking about when he bids us pray for revival? When I was in Sunday school I was taught a chorus about prayer that went like this: "A little talk with Jesus makes it right, all right." I do not mean to belittle those brief, quiet moments that we spend with Jesus at any time during the day, but that is not the kind of praying that ushers in revival.

Revival praying is intensive praying, passionate praying, prolonged praying—praying that holds on to God like Jacob when he prayed: "I will not let you go unless you bless me" (Gen. 32:26).

The prophet Isaiah gives us a picture of watchmen standing on the walls of Jerusalem crying out to God and reminding him of his promises concerning the Holy City: "I have posted watchmen on your walls, O Jerusalem; they will never be silent day or night. You who call on the LORD, give yourselves no rest, and give him no rest till he establishes Jerusalem and makes her the praise of the earth" (Isa. 62:6–7). The men were to give God no rest until Jerusalem was restored to its former glory.

Revival praying is not just ordinary praying. It is unhurried praying, not just saying words with a breathless eagerness to get it finished. It is passionate praying—prayer that is not afraid to draw upon one's emotions, to cry out to God, with tears if that is the way one feels. Far too often our prayers run along these lines: "Please excuse me from the Upper Room, but call me when the fire falls."

I heard one preacher say that this kind of praying (what I am calling revival praying) reminded him of his mother, who had a habit of losing her keys. When this happened she would turn the house upside down until she found them. There would be intense searching until they were found. Everything else stopped in the house, and everyone was enlisted in the task. Nothing else mattered at that moment other than finding those keys. Someone has said that "we will not see revival until we can't live without it."

God goes further in this matter of prayer.

"And Seek My Face"

If we are honest we are often more interested in seeing the hand of God at work than we are in seeing his face. We want to see the sick healed, we want to see supernatural events taking place—desires that are perfectly right and proper. But revival praying puts as its priority a new vision of God, a new understanding of him; to know God for who he is, and not just for what he can give. Revival praying is where we are drawn into a new relationship with him, where intimacy with God becomes the most important thing.

When did you last get down before God and pray with fervor and passion? And with a desire not simply to see a spiritual renaissance but to know God more deeply, to see his face? That's the kind of praying that brings revival.

Thus, the second reason why revival tarries is:

We do not pray enough, we do not pray passionately enough, not perseveringly enough, not persistently enough.

Is there a prayer group for revival in your church? If not, join one that might be in the area, or you could start one.

CHAPTER 5

BLOCKS TO REVIVAL

We said earlier when we talked about divine sovereignty that God takes action to answer prayer when he sees fit, at his own pace, and in his own good time. Yet as we have seen there are things we can do at the present moment to bring revival nearer, such as humbling ourselves, praying more sincerely, specifically, and passionately. But now God has a further challenge for us—he asks us to turn from our wicked ways.

"If my people who are called by my name shall humble themselves and pray and seek my face and turn from their wicked ways"

The people of God with wicked ways? Surely it means silly ways, careless ways perhaps. The Bible says "wicked ways," and *wicked,* I imagine, is not a word we like applied to ourselves. The word *ways* suggests behavior that has become settled and established.

Young people nowadays tend to use the word *wicked* in quite a different way from its dictionary meaning. A great film or an exciting event can be "wicked," but I assure you when God uses the word he means it to be understood in its original sense—"sinful and iniquitous."

What Are "Wicked Ways"?

What are these Spirit-quenching things that block the path to revival? Well, God is not specific about them, so we are left to some degree of speculation in regard to their precise nature. Permit me to give you some examples based on Scripture of what I think can be listed as the wicked ways of the people of God.

When we allow our spiritual condition to remain lukewarm and complacent—that is a wicked way. Jesus had some searing words to say to the church in Laodicea about their lukewarm condition. "I know your deeds, that you are neither cold nor hot. I wish you were either one or the other! So, because you are lukewarm—neither hot nor cold—I am about to spit you out of my mouth" (Rev. 3:15–16).

When we hold bitterness and resentment against a group or an individual and refuse to offer the same degree of forgiveness that Christ has given to us—that is a wicked way. Unforgiveness kills the spiritual life; it is like drinking poison and expecting the other person to die. Jesus said those who will not forgive will not be forgiven (Matt. 6:14).

When by our disunity we present to the world a fragmented picture of the face of

Christ—that is a wicked way. How snobbish one church can be with another! Some churches would rather die in separation than live in fellowship. Denominationalism—believing your denomination or group is better than another—is an impediment to the spiritual life. God doesn't necessarily want to take you out of your denomination, but I believe he does want to take the denomination out of you. (See our Lord's prayer in John 17.)

When we neglect the reading and study of the Scriptures—that is a wicked way. God has given us just one book—the Bible. It is his one and only published work. How much time do we spend in it? And do we really believe it? Do you know that the majority of Christians admit that they have not read every word in God's Book, while readily admitting to reading every word in other books they peruse.

When we withhold our tithes and offerings from God—that is a wicked way. It is a sobering truth when God's people realize they are guilty of robbing God. It's hypocritical to describe a thief or a robber as "wicked" when we ourselves may be in that same category spiritually speaking. "Will a man rob God?" (Mal. 3:8).

Nor is this all! What about such things as continued moral failure, lying, low expectations of holiness in oneself and others, indifference to the winning of others to Christ, loss of temper, idolatry, gossip, hypocrisy, pretense . . . the list could go on and on. Is it any wonder why revival does not come when there are so many wicked things among us! Charles Finney once said, "Christians are more to blame for not being revived than sinners are for not being converted."

Some of the things listed above might not be seen as serious in worldly people. But God's own people—people claiming to have the life of Christ in them, to be new creatures? If we are in Christ and Christ is in us, then the world has a right to expect us to be different.

What Do We Do About Our Wicked Ways?

God says we are to turn from them. What does that mean? A synonym for the word *turn* is *repent*. Some Christians may feel that deciding to discontinue what God calls wicked ways is enough. It is not. Once we admit that we are in need of change in our lives, there must be a moment of deep repentance before we can move on in our relationship with God.

To recognize something as wrong and resolving not to do it again is good but not good enough. We must take care of past violations by repenting of them. There can be no deep, ongoing relationship with the Lord until we know how to act over the wrongs of the past.

When our Lord spoke to the church at Ephesus, he reprimanded them because they had left their first love (Rev. 2:4). How was the situation to be corrected? They were to remember from where they had fallen, repent, and return. Someone has described this as the Three Rs of

Relationship. They were to look back to the position from which they had fallen, repent of it, and return to God in deep humility of heart.

What Does the Bible Say?

The Bible is replete with texts that stress the importance of repentance.

> If you repent, I will restore you that you may serve me.
>
> **Jeremiah 15:19**

> Therefore say to the house of Israel, "This is what the Sovereign LORD says: Repent! Turn from your idols and renounce all your detestable practices!"
>
> **Ezekiel 14:6**

> From that time on Jesus began to preach, "Repent, for the kingdom of heaven is near."
>
> **Matthew 4:17**

> They went out and preached that people should repent. They drove out many

demons and anointed many sick people
with oil and healed them.

Mark 6:12

Peter replied, "Repent and be baptized,
every one of you, in the name of Jesus
Christ for the forgiveness of your sins.
And you will receive the gift of the Holy
Spirit. The promise is for you and your
children and for all who are far off—for
all whom the Lord our God will call."

Acts 2:38–39

In the past God overlooked such igno-
rance, but now he commands all people
everywhere to repent. For he has set a day
when he will judge the world with justice
by the man he has appointed. He has
given proof of this to all men by raising
him from the dead.

Acts 17:30

Turning in a New Direction

Repentance, however, is one of the most mis-
understood words in the Christian vocabulary.

People think repentance is feeling sorry for your sins. But that is not what the word is about. The Greek word for repentance is *metanoia*, which means "a change of mind." It is good when we feel sorry for our "wicked ways," but that is the outcome of repentance, not the beginning of it. Repentance is seeing that the direction in which you are going is wrong, then turning in a new direction with your thoughts, changing your mind, for example, about where your life is found.

The biggest mistake people make about repentance is that they expect to feel sorry about their sin before they repent. Repentance begins not by waiting to feel sorry about our sin but by seeing how wrong it is and making up our minds to turn in a new direction. It begins with a change of mind, for when the mind is changed, then our feelings feel the impact of that. Our feelings follow our thoughts in the same way that ducklings follow their mother on a pond.

So don't think that because you don't have any deep feelings of sorrow or any guilty feelings that you are not required to repent. Don't wait for your feelings to be stirred. What we think about affects the way we feel. You take the first step, and the feelings will follow—don't worry about them. Do what is right, and the rest will follow on as night follows day.

A Conditional Promise

But what if we do what God asks? Listen once again:

> If my people, who are called by my name,
> will humble themselves and pray and
> seek my face and turn from their wicked
> ways, then will I hear from heaven and
> will forgive their sin and will heal their
> land.

What a promise! God will hear, forgive, and heal.

Go over every word carefully.

He will *hear*. He *listens* to us when we pray. C. H. Spurgeon used to say that prayer is like pulling on the ropes here on earth, which causes a bell to ring in heaven. Do you believe God hears us praying for revival? I mean *really* believe? Well, not to believe it is to make God a liar.

He will hear *from heaven*. We need to be reminded over and over again that it is from heaven that true revival comes. It is beyond our power to usher in revival by our human methods, much as we would like to do so. Only God himself by his own quickening visitation can renew.

He will *forgive our sin*. Isn't this a most amazing thing? Even though we have impeded his grace and quenched his Spirit for years, the moment we turn and ask for his forgiveness, he gives it to us fully and freely.

He will *heal our land*. The reference here is clearly to the physical land, as can be seen from the verse preceding this where God says that in judgment on his people's sins he will shut up the heavens and send locusts to devour the land. The "land" that we possess as Christians, however, is not a physical inheritance but a spiritual one. Neglect ravages it and causes it to rot, but

God can restore what has been lost in ways above and beyond our thinking.

Well, there it is.

The reasons why revival tarries (from the human side at least) are:

- We are stuck in our pride.
- We do not pray enough, passionately enough, and sincerely enough.
- We are reluctant to turn from our wicked ways and genuinely repent.

What Are You Going to Do About It?

It is a lot to believe that we can witness a turn of the spiritual tide in our land when we see Christianity declining and thousands drifting away from the mainline churches, but we must put our whole weight upon it. We must humble ourselves before God, pray more in private and in groups, claim the help of God to cut out everything in our lives of which he disapproves, plead for his grace, and ask him to flood our churches with his power.

Are you willing to pray more and join a group praying for revival, or to start a prayer meeting? You can be sure of this: God would not call us to pray if our situation were unredeemable.

It would be wonderful if the whole church throughout our land would heed this message, but the history of revival shows that when a proportion of God's people meets his conditions he moves in answer to their prayers. In Wales God used a small praying group to usher in revival. You could be the vanguard of a mighty move of the Holy Spirit if you are willing to pay the price.

Drawing closer to God in the way I have described may not guarantee we see corporate revival (that must be left to God's sovereignty). But one thing is sure: *you yourself will be revived.* And your action along with others will bring us closer to the great outpouring of the Holy Spirit for which so many are longing.

CHAPTER 6

A REVIVED CHURCH

What Will a Revived Church Look Like?

The church of Jesus Christ will shine with a new light when revival comes. Denominationalism—already beginning to be broken down—will, in the flow of revival power, be broken down completely. In revival, people are not inclined to say, "I am an Anglican," "I am a Baptist," "I am a Methodist," or "I am a Pentecostal." Those attitudes dissolve in the river of God's Spirit.

In revival times God acts quickly; his work accelerates. The early church operating in the power of the Holy Spirit saw eight thousand people converted within a few weeks (Acts 4:4; 5:14). When Paul left Thessalonica after just a few weeks of ministry, he left behind him a virile church whose quality can be gauged from 1 Thessalonians 1:3. No wonder he asked them to pray that "the message of the Lord may spread rapidly and be honored, just as it was with you" (2 Thess. 3:1). The truth of the gospel makes rapid strides in times of revival. People are born again and grow quickly at such times.

Holiness, another characteristic of revival, will add a sharper edge to Christian living, bringing a clearer line of demarcation between the church and the world. Love flowing between believers will show itself in ways that defy human analysis and cause unbelievers to say, "How much they love one another."

Yet another characteristic of a church in revival is a responsiveness to God's Word. A powerful sense of God's presence imparts new authority to the truth of his Word. Whereas before, the Word of God made only a superficial impact, now it searches the hearts of the hearers to the depth of their being. At Pentecost, and for several decades afterwards, the Word of God touched the hearts of people in a dynamic way. The apostle Paul thanked God that when the Thessalonians heard the Word of God, they accepted it not as from men but as the very Word of God (1 Thess. 2:13).

Duncan Campbell describes the condition of the church during the revival that took place in the Hebrides in this way:

> I would first like to state what I mean by revival as witnessed in the Hebrides. I do not mean a time of religious entertainment, with crowds gathering to enjoy an evening of bright gospel singing; I do not mean sensational or spectacular advertising. I do not mean high-pressure methods to get men and women to an enquiry room—in revival every service is an enquiry room; the road and hillside become sacred spots to many when the

winds of God blow. Revival is a going of
God among His people, and an awareness
of God laying hold of the community . . .
the fear of God lays hold upon the community, moving men and women, who
until then had no concern for spiritual
things.[1]

Listen also to his description of a scene that
took place during the first days of the movement
of the Spirit in the Hebrides.

A crowded church, the service is over: the
congregation, reluctant to disperse, stand
outside the church in a silence that is
tense. Suddenly a cry is heard within: a
young man, burdened for the souls of
his fellow-men, is pouring out his soul
in intercession. He prays until he falls
into a trance and lies prostrate on the
floor of the church . . . the congregation,
moved by a power they could not resist,
came back into the church, and a wave
of conviction of sin swept over the gath-
ering, moving strong men to cry to God
for mercy. This service continued until

the small hours of the morning, but so great was the distress and so deep the hunger which gripped men and women, that they refused to go home, and already were assembling in another part of the parish. A feature of this early morning visitation was the number who made their way to the church, moved by a power they had not experienced before: others were deeply convicted of their sin and crying for mercy, in their own homes, before ever coming near the church.[2]

Revival Will Affect the Nation

Revival in the church has always had an ethical and evangelistic overflow into the world, often of great power. In terms of evangelism it is the spiritual fulfillment of what happened in the postexilic restoration: "This is what the LORD Almighty says: 'In those days ten men from all languages and nations will take firm hold of one Jew by the hem of his robe and say, "Let us go with you, because we have heard that God is with you"'" (Zech. 8:23).

Our nation needs God—that is for sure. We are slipping into apostasy, sin is rampant and rife, young people have no clear ethical guidelines, postmodernism rules in our colleges and universities, moral absolutes no longer prevail, there is an undermining of so many things. How can we reach them if there is no revival? How can things change?

We can't look to the nation to correct itself morally on its own. The answer to our morality does not lie entirely in the chambers of government but in the house of God.

How would revival influence our nation? One of the best answers to that question was given by Dr. W. E. Sangster. One Monday morning in the mid-1950s, the nation woke up to read in a number of national papers the substance of a sermon preached by him the previous day. Some newspapers printed the main points of his sermon on their front pages. His theme was: "Revival: The Need and the Way."[3]

Sangster raised the question: What would a revival of religion do for Britain? He gave the following ten answers:

1. It would pay old debts.

He pointed out that in the days of the Welsh revival those who dismissed it as a wave of emotional fanaticism changed their minds when they heard that wherever the revival went people were paying old and neglected debts. "A lifting of common morality," he said, "is an early and inevitable consequence of born-again religion."

2. It would reduce sexual immorality.

Quoting from *English Life and Leisure,* Sangster said there were 10,000 prostitutes in London alone and 250,000 men were estimated to make use of them every week. (Nowadays, those figures have doubled.) This foul traffic, he claimed, was an offence to God and while figures and complaints could do nothing, a revival of religion would. Men and women touched by the Holy Spirit would learn that in God there is power to obey the commandments of God.

3. It would disinfect the theater and the press.

The Christian faith has never had a quarrel with drama as such, claimed Sangster, but it is deeply concerned when the stage is misused for the deliberate inflaming of lust. Our newspapers include some of the best in the world and some of the worst. Those in the latter class are so sex-sodden that they come close to pornography. In Sangster's day television was in its infancy. What would he say about some of today's programs that are peppered with four-letter words and portray scenes that are an offense to decency and civility? A revival of religion would cause men and women to turn from such things.

4. It would cut the divorce rate.

In the 1950s divorces ran at a much lower rate than they do today. The texture of society gets flabby, said Sangster, when divorce gets common. Young people who enter marriage with their eye on the backdoor and say to themselves, "Well, if it doesn't work out I can always get a divorce," make for it when things get difficult more quickly than they think they will.

Those who pray together are more likely to stay together.

5. It would reduce juvenile crime.

It was in the 1950s that the "adolescent thug" began to appear. And the cause? Without doubt, the breakdown in family life. It is rare indeed that a thug comes out of a Christian home. It can happen, and sometimes does, but not often. No one is safe in goodness unless he or she wants to be good, said Sangster. And what makes people want to be good? Faith in Christ.

6. It would lessen the prison population.

In the United Kingdom the prison population in the 1930s stood around 15,000. In the 1950s it was 20,000. Now, in the first decade of the twenty-first century it is getting close to 75,000. Is there not some connection between the fact that as churches have been emptying our prisons have been filling? Sangster claimed that in his day the moral capital built up by generations of God-fearing people was nearing exhaustion. Were he alive today, he would see that it has become bankrupt. Only a revival of the Christian faith can turn the tide.

7. It would improve the quality and increase the output of work.

The Christian faith makes a difference to work. How? Because a man or woman who is committed to Jesus Christ works not just for wages but for God. Men and women need wages, of course, since no one can live without money, but the highest motivation to work and to do a task well is to do it for God.

8. It would restore to the nation a sense of high destiny.

During the "Empire" days the British people believed they had a special and high destiny in the world, but some aspects of the idea were somewhat foolish. Thankfully much of that imperial pride has gone. What is our destiny in today's world? We still have an important role in world affairs, but how much more powerful that role would be if it were energized by the stands of biblical faith.

9. It would make us invincible in the war of ideas.

In Sangster's day the war of ideas was between communism and capitalism. Both creeds had their passionate proponents, some even willing to die for their cause. Sangster pointed out that the real war in the war of ideas is whether or not there is a God, whether a person is what he eats, and whether the last explanation of the universe is material or spiritual. The Christian faith has a secret that no other ideology knows—how to die to self. The finest schemes fail on the selfishness of mankind. The possession and practice of that secret would make us invincible in the war of ideas.

10. It would give happiness and peace to the people.

Throughout time men and women have sought to find peace in their hearts. But peace can be found only in a relationship with the Prince of Peace—the Lord Jesus Christ himself. Almost the only hope of happiness for many today is to win something big on the lottery. The Christian faith offers a peace that does not depend on circumstances. Wars may rage around us, but peace can stay with us—if the peace we have is from God.[4]

Britain, said Sangster, speaking in the 1950s, has many needs, but her greatest is revival. Today, close on five decades later, the needs of our world are much greater and our greatest need is still revival.

We have watched our country slipping back for a generation. And without doubt complacency and lukewarmness gnaw at the door of the church. It is a lot to believe that humility, believing prayer, radical repentance, and cutting out everything God does not want in our lives can change things, but not to believe it would make God a liar.

God longs for revival more than we do. "Return to me, and I will return to you," he said in Malachi 3:7.

May the Sleeping Giant Wake Up

Let's not settle for the spiritual status quo, a mediocre, weak, and anemic brand of Christianity, when God wants to make available to us the same kind of power that energized the early church. Dr. Martyn Lloyd-Jones said on one occasion that the Christian church is like a sleeping giant. If that is so, then it is time for it to wake up.

There have been two great spiritual awakenings that have affected Britain in the last five hundred years. One was the Reformation in the middle of the sixteenth century, triggered by that great reformer, Martin Luther. The second was the Evangelical Awakening in the eighteenth century under such men as John Wesley, George Whitfield, and others. Now in the twenty-first century we are ready for a third awakening, one that will turn the tide and make the church once again the power God intends it to be.

To absorb ideas about revival costs nothing, but to enter into revival costs everything—our time and changes in our behavior. We shall be very guilty, if having come to understand revival and be convinced of its need, we then do nothing about it. Let us report for duty in the battle for our nation's soul.

Let the prayer of Isaiah become our prayer. "Oh, that you would rend the heavens and come down, that the mountains would tremble before you! . . . come down to make your name known to your enemies and cause the nations to quake before you!" (Isa. 64:1–2).

Whatever the needs of the church and the nation, our greatest need is revival.

Hear the merciful promise of our heavenly Father once again:

> If my people, who are called by my name,
> will humble themselves and pray and
> seek my face and turn from their wicked
> ways, then will I hear from heaven and
> will forgive their sin and will heal their
> land. (2 Chron. 7:14)

How You Can Start

Would you join me in this personal prayer?

Heavenly Father,
I come to you in Jesus' name . . .
Search my heart at this moment
and expose any wicked ways that may be
    in me.
I want to be the person you want me
    to be.
I repent of the wrongs in my life;
show them to me whatever they are—
lukewarmness, indifference to the lost,
lack of prayer, lack of passionate prayer,
neglect of the Bible, compromise,
    resentment toward others, pride.
O God, forgive me for my pride.
I renounce it and turn from it now in
    your presence.
I bundle all these things together
and bring them to the foot of the cross.
I receive your forgiveness.
Help me to start afresh this day.
Change me by your grace,
forgive me and restore me,
set my heart on fire for you,

that I will be unafraid to witness to my
    friends and family.
May I never be ashamed of you.
Send revival to the land . . .
and start the work in me.
In Jesus' name I pray.
Amen.

Notes

Chapter 1

1. James I. Packer, *God in the Midst* (Milton Keynes: Word Publishing, 1987).
2. Ibid.
3. Duncan Campbell, *God's Answer: Revival Sermons* (Edinburgh: The Faith Mission, 1960).
4. Ibid.

Chapter 2

1. W. E. Sangster, *The Craft of Sermon Construction* (London: Epworth Press, 1949).
2. W. E. Sangster, *Revival: The Need and the Way*, Pamphlet (London: Epworth Press, 1957).

Chapter 3

1. C. S. Lewis, *Mere Christianity* (London: Macmillan Publishing Co., 1943).

2. Charles Swindoll, *Strengthening Your Grip* (Milton Keynes: Word Publishing, 1982).

Chapter 4

1. W. E. Sangster, *The Pure in Heart* (London: Epworth Press, 1954).

Chapter 6

1. Duncan Campbell, *God's Answer: Revival Sermons* (Edinburgh: The Faith Mission, April 1960).

2. Ibid.

3. W. E. Sangster, *Revival: The Need and the Way*, Pamphlet (London: Epworth Press, 1957).

4. Ibid.